OCH WHEESHT AND GET OAN WAE IT

Published by Jumped Up Publishing in association with Summersdale.

Bookspeed, 16 Salamander Yards, Edinburgh EH6 7DD
Tel: 0131 467 8100
Fax: 0131 467 8008
sales@bookspeed.com
www.bookspeed.com

Printed and bound in the Czech Republic

ISBN: 978-0-95536-411-2

Disclaimer
Every effort has been made to attribute the quotations in this collection to the correct source. Should there be any omissions or errors in this respect we apologise and shall be pleased to make the appropriate acknowledgements in any future edition.

OCH
WHEESHT
AND
GET OAN
WAE IT

bookspeed

You'll have had yer tea...

Scottish saying

Every man dies. Not every
man really lives.

William Wallace

There shall be a Scottish
Parliament. I like that.

**Donald Dewar (1937–2000),
Inaugural First Minister of Scotland**

Mony a mickle maks a muckle!

(Saving a small amount soon builds to a large amount.)

Ne'er cast a clout till
May be out.

*(Don't throw your winter
clothes out until the end
of May.)*

Black as the Earl of
Hell's waistcoat!

Scottish saying

He's that tight he would peel
an orange in his pocket!

Yer aff yer heid.

(You're a little bit daft.)

Do you know what type of
lighting they used on Noah's
ark? Flood lighting.

Chic Murray

Work as if you live in
the early days of a
better nation.

Alasdair Gray

Dinna test the depth o'
the burn wi' baith feet.

Dreams do come true, if we only wish hard enough. You can have everything in life as long as you will sacrifice everything else for it.

J. M. Barrie

Dinnae teach yer
Granny tae suck eggs.

A thread will tie an honest
man better than a chain
a rogue.

This is Glasgow, we'll
just set aboot ye.

Smeato (aka John Smeaton,
Glasgow Airport Baggage Handler)

Me and other folks were just
tryin' tae get the boot in
and some other guy
banjoed him.

Smeato

Speak o' the Devil!
(and he's sure to appear).

Scottish saying

Never show your teeth
unless you can bite.

Our business in this world
is not to succeed, but
to continue to fail in
good spirits.

Robert Louis Stevenson

Yer gey peely
wally looking.

(You don't look very well.)

My parents used to take me
to the pet department and
tell me it was a zoo.

Billy Connolly

To marry is to halve
your rights and double
your duties.

Sandy was only five feet
tall. He reckoned it was
due to his diet as a child:
condensed milk and
shortbread.

The Scots have an
infallible cure for sea-
sickness. They lean
over the side of the
ship with a ten-pence
coin in their teeth.

Toilet out of order.
Please use floor below.

Notice in an office in Edinburgh

It is tremendously good fun winding up the Scots. It is terribly easy, particularly Scottish politicians. They can take things far too seriously.

Jeremy Paxman, English broadcaster and author

Anger is more hurtful
than the wrong that
caused it.

Kilts aren't the most
comfortable thing to wear if
the wind's blowing.

Dougray Scott, film actor

Better keep the devil
at the door than have
to turn him out of
the house.

A good gulp of whisky at
bedtime – it's not scientific
but it helps [as a cure
for a cold].

Sir Alexander Fleming (1881–
1955), discoverer of penicillin,
recipient of the Nobel Prize in
Physiology or Medicine, 1945

They say the Scots
have a good sense of
humour; that's only
because it's free!

Oh, what a tangled
web we weave,
When first we practise
to deceive!

Sir Walter Scott

The medicine that
hurts the most is
generally the
best healer.

In Scotland there is no such thing as bad weather – only the wrong clothes.

Never trust a man who when
left alone with a tea cosy…
doesn't try it on.

Billy Connolly

It's niver lost what a
freend gets.

*(What you give to a friend,
is not lost to you.)*

If your breasts are too big,
you may fall over… unless
you wear a rucksack.

Ivor Cutler

A bad wound may
heal but a bad
name will kill.

What we, the Scots, do
is stoicism with an air of
disgruntlement. That is our
failsafe coping mechanism.
We're good at it.

**Gary Sutherland, journalist
and author**

Wide ears and short
tongues are best.

Dae ye think ah button up the back?

(I would appreciate it if you would stop talking nonsense.)

Cheer up hen and hae a bit
o ma oamlette.

Fat Boab fae Kilbarchan

A friend is a gift you
give yourself.

Robert Louis Stevenson

Dinnae fash.

(Don't worry.)

Ell hae twa paes and an ingin in an' a'.

(I'll have two pies and an onion one as well.)

Hungry Dundonian on match day

Never let your feet run faster
than your shoes.

Wilful waste makes
woeful want.

For which impertinence I
received a mighty buffet!

Ivor Cutler

See-uz ma bumpers.

*(Would you be so kind
as to pass me my
slippers please.)*

Alexander Mair

To cultivate an English
accent is already a
departure away from
what you are.

Sean Connery

Yer bum's oot
the windae.

(You're just messing about.)

He sclaffed the baw and it
skyted out of the ground and
away down Gorgie Road.

Football pundit from Scotsport

Those who bring
sunshine into the lives of
others cannot keep it
from themselves.

J. M. Barrie

Git yer hauns aff ma yelly banany.

(Please don't touch my yellow banana.)

Edinburgh resident and former Bookspeed employee

Choose your wife with
her nightcap on!

He was going at it like a
baggy up a Border burn.

Bill McLaren

Here Ina, check oot his shang-a-langs!

(Would you take a look at that young man's flared trousers!)

Alexander Mair

Luck never gives,
it only lends.

Dae ye think ah came up the Clyde in a banana skin?

(Do you think I'm stupid?)

A liar shou'd always hae
a good memory.

Feart? Naw ah'm nae feart.

(Scared? I'm not scared.)

There are two seasons in
Scotland: June and winter.

Billy Connolly

Keep your fears to yourself,
but share your courage
with others.

Robert Louis Stevenson

We look to Scotland
for all our ideas
of civilisation.

Voltaire

There's daggers in
men's smiles.

Shakespeare, *Macbeth*

Don't judge each day by the
harvest you reap, but by
the seeds you plant.

Robert Louis Stevenson

Enough is as good
as a feast.

Patient: If I give up drink,
tobacco and sex will
I live longer?
Doctor: No, It'll only
seem like it.

Chic Murray

He's as welcome as water in
a holed ship.

We're a' Jock
Tamson's bairns!

(We are all God's children.)

Yer like a hauf
shut knife.

(You look depressed.)

Fair fa' your honest,
sonsie face,
Great chieftain o' the
puddin-race!

Robert Burns

They talk of ma'
drinkin' but niver
ma thurst.

It is not real work unless
you would rather be doing
something else.

J. M. Barrie

Away and cuddle
my humph.

*(A response to an
outlandish request.)*

Alan Laing's mother

Cruellest lies are often
told in silence.

Robert Louis Stevenson

Ye canny whack it.

(You can't beat it.)

If I had a dog as daft,
I would shoot him.

Temper is a weapon that we
hold only by the blade.

J. M. Barrie

A wild goose never
laid tame eggs.

It's got me fair
scunnered.

(It's got me very annoyed.)

Scottish expression

Gonnae no dae that...

The lighthouse keepers from
Chewing the Fat

He is well tidy by
the way.

*(I rather fancy that nice
young chap.)*

Young Scottish lass

I was makin' tea in my
pyjamas. I must remember
to buy a teapot.

Chic Murray

Have you heard the rumour
that the Grand Canyon was
started by a Scotsman who
lost a coin in a ditch?

Shut yer pus.

(Shut your mouth.)

Scottish expression

Danger and delight
grow from one stalk.

I fear that the development
of the railways will
destroy the need
for waterproof coats.

Charles Macintosh

To travel hopefully is a
better thing than to arrive.

Robert Louis Stevenson

A dish of married love
grows soon cold.

There's nae pockets
in a shroud.

*(You don't need money
when you're dead.)*

Scottish saying

And he gubbed him wae
an ashtray… oan the
Ballachulish ferry.

Billy Connolly

She's got mair faces than
the toon clock!

Yer face is trippin' ye!

(You look unhappy.)

Scottish expression

This party, the Scottish party, the national party, carries your hope. We shall carry it carefully and make the nation proud.

Alex Salmond upon being re-elected First Minister, 6 May 2011

He was a bold man
who first ate a Haggis.

A day to come seems longer
than a year that's gone.

Ye make a better door
than ya dae a windae.

*(Said to someone who is
blocking your view.)*

It's bra is it!

(I think it's rather good.)

A Dundonian

Look to the living, love them,
and hold on.

Douglas Dunn

Twelve highlanders
and a bagpipe make
a rebellion.

Roses are red, violets are blue, I'm a schizophrenic, and so am I.

Billy Connolly

He wis tawkin' pure
mince by the way.

(He was talking rubbish.)

Scottish saying

It's a braw, bricht moonlicht
nicht the nicht.

Anonymous

Fa's yer doos?

(How is it going there?)

Doric

Where's Uganda? Buried
next to ma granda.

Chic Murray

Angus called in to see his friend Donald to find he was stripping the wallpaper from the walls. Rather obviously, he remarked, 'You're decorating, I see,' to which Donald replied, 'Naw. I'm movin' house.'

Poor is the triumph
o'er the timid hare!

James Thomson

Aye, he's the high
heid yin.

(Yes, he is the boss.)

Facts are chiels that
winna ding.

Robert Burns

Be happy while you're livin', 'cause yer a lang time deed.

(Enjoy today because life is short.)

For years I thought
the club's name was
Partick Thistle Nil.

Billy Connolly

KILT, n. A costume
sometimes worn by
Scotsmen in America and
Americans in Scotland.

Ambrose Bierce

Confessed faults are
half mended.

I walked into the bedroom.
The curtains were drawn but
the furniture was real.

Chic Murray

Never marry for
money, ye'll borrow
it cheaper.

Marriage: a friendship
recognised by
the police.

Robert Louis Stevenson

In some Scottish restaurants
they heat the knives so you
can't use too much butter.

Never drink whisky with water and never drink water without whisky.

Scottish proverb

There are no foreign
lands. It is the
traveller only who
is foreign.

Robert Louis Stevenson

It is rumoured that the entire
population of Aberdeen took
to the streets with an empty
glass in their hands when
the weather forecaster
said there would be a
nip in the air.

Gut nae fish till ye
get them.

*(Scottish equivalent of
'Don't count your chickens
until they hatch.')*

How do you persuade
a Scotsman to go on
the roof? Tell him
the drinks are on
the house.

Scottish joke

Life is not a matter of
holding good cards, but of
playing a poor hand well.

Robert Louis Stevenson

I will go anywhere,
provided it is forward.

David Livingstone

A fool may earn money, but
it takes a wise man
to keep it.

Hope is brightest
when it dawns
from fears.

Sir Walter Scott

Marriage is a wonderful
invention: then again, so is
a bicycle repair kit.

Billy Connolly

He's got paralysis of
the calluses.

It is not in doing what you
like, but liking what you
do that is the secret
of happiness.

J. M. Barrie

He's fair mingin'.

(He's not very attractive.)

Concentrate all your thoughts upon the work in hand. The sun's rays only burn when focussed.

A. G. Bell

A deaf Scotsman will hear
tha clink o' money.

Ah dinnae bile ma
cabbages twice.

Have you heard the
joke about Rothesay?
Yes, it's a bute.

Chic Murray

A' geese are
nae swans.

Doric proverb

Ooosha min' tak aboot
needin' a paddle fae
that dingie.

London is the devil's
drawing room.

Tobias Smollett

An advertisement in an
Edinburgh newspaper
read, *'For sale. Genuine
leopard-skin coat.
Spotless condition.'*

Scottish joke

Ye'll hae yer heid in
yer hands to play with.

For God's sake, give me the
young man who has brains
enough to make a fool
of himself.

Robert Louis Stevenson

What cannot be cured
must be endured.

Awa' an' bile yer heid.

(Don't be so ridiculous.)

Love may not make the
world go round, but I must
admit that it makes the
ride worthwhile.

Sean Connery

The power of
imagination makes
us infinite.

John Muir

A house without a dog, a
cat, or a little child is
a house without joy
or laughter.

Yer maw's a baw and yer
faither's wan an' aw.

Wendy English

Ma heid's mince.

(My head is a little mixed up.)

Does your boyfriend ever discuss UNO? God, he never talks about anything else!

Chic Murray

Better to bend than
to break.

Perfect love cannot be
without equality.

I've always wanted to go to
Switzerland to see what the
army does with those
wee red knives.

Billy Connolly

Opera is where a guy
gets stabbed in the
back, and instead of
dying, he sings.

Robert Burns

There is no duty we so
much underrate as the duty
of being happy.

Robert Louis Stevenson

Keep the heid.

(Stay calm, don't get upset.)

Whit's fur ye'll no go by ye.

Scottish saying

www.bookspeed.com

OCH WHEESHT AND GET OAN WAE IT